The People's Friend

It's a Wonderful Life!

A smile for each day of 2014

To Alistair + Mary
Wishing you a good Christmas

DC Thomson   Belle x

Published 2014 by Waverley Books,
144 Port Dundas Road, Glasgow, G4 0HZ

A catalogue entry for this book is available from the British
Library.

ISBN 978-1-84535-507-4

Printed and bound in China.

The People's Friend

Laughter is good for you! If you enjoy wordplay, slapstick, stand-up comics, or whatever else tickles your funny bone, and if you enjoy sharing jokes with your friends and family, young and old, then this book is for you. Put together with *The People's Friend* reader in mind, and presented as a-smile-a-day book, *It's a Wonderful Life!* contains punchy one-liners, wise and wry pithy comments, and little stories to make you smile throughout the year.

We hope this book will make you smile and help you to take on new challenges and live life to the full. As Charlie Chaplin once said, "A day without laughter is a day wasted."

"I'll need a cat in this shade."

January

❧ Wednesday January 1

Hospitality is making your guests feel at home, even if you wish they were.

❧ Thursday January 2

Our neighbour's son was attending university away from home, and as a student he fell into the familiar pattern of going to lectures, studying in the library, working on essays, eating pasta and rice, sleeping occasionally, and forgetting to call or write home.

Then one day he found this letter on his doormat:

"Dear Mark, Mum and I – well – we both loved your last letter home. But of course, we were much younger then."

❧ Friday January 3

Why is it that when you tidy out the garage, you throw away something exactly four weeks before you need it?

❧ Saturday January 4

Never test the depth of water with both feet.

❧ Sunday January 5

Always remember that you're unique. Just like everyone else.

❧ Monday January 6

Helen: John darling, that awful woman next door has bought herself a new dress exactly like mine. It's really not on.
John: Is that a cleverly disguised hint that you need a new dress?
Helen: Well, it would be a cheaper than moving to a new house!

❧ Tuesday January 7

Grandpa was getting really quite deaf. The doctor arranged for him to get hearing aids and they made a huge difference.

He went back for an assessment and the doctor declared, "Your hearing is so much improved. Your family must be really pleased."

Grandpa replied, "Oh, I haven't told them yet. I just listen. I'm changing my will!"

❧ Wednesday January 8

You know you are getting on a bit when you see the toys you played with as a child forming a museum display.

❧ Thursday January 9

Keep your dreams alive – hit the "snooze" button.

❧ Friday January 10

Teacher: Tommy, why do you always get so dirty?
Tommy: Well, I'm a lot closer to the ground than you are.

❧ Saturday January 11

Why is it that the dishwasher works perfectly well as soon as the engineer arrives?

❧ Sunday January 12

The computer beat me at chess, but it was no match for me at kick-boxing.

❧ Monday January 13

When Mum says, "It's your decision", what she really means is, "The right decision should be obvious to you by now."

✿ Tuesday January 14

With so many demands from all of us, Mum was getting a bit tetchy. She eventually blew a fuse:

"I can please only one person each day. Today is not your day. Tomorrow isn't looking good either."

✿ Wednesday January 15

It is embarrassing eating out with my Dad. He loves to joke, so every time someone in a restaurant drops a glass or a plate, he shouts "Sack the juggler!"

✿ Thursday January 16

I asked Grandpa why he liked sitting in his armchair so much:

"Well, if you have lived a good life like I have, when you get older, you can just think back and enjoy it the second time around."

⁂ Friday January 17

Why is it that when I do something good, no one remembers, but when I do something wrong, no one forgets?

⁂ Saturday January 18

No, I didn't say it was your fault. I said I was blaming you.

⁂ Sunday January 19

In the Main Street Church Bulletin:

"The Parish Church Outreach Programme now has thirty volunteers whose job it is to call on people who are not currently afflicted with any church."

⁂ Monday January 20

I wondered why the cricket ball was getting bigger.
  Then it hit me.

❧ Tuesday January 21

Grandpa was rocking in his chair. I asked him about when he first met Granny.

He thought, and rocked, and then he said, "When I first met your grandmother, she said I only had two faults. Everything I said and everything I did."

❧ Wednesday January 22

A husband should always forget his mistakes. There's no point in two people remembering the same things.

❧ Thursday January 23

It was Martin and Amelia's first wedding anniversary.

Martin says to Amelia, "Let's go out and have some fun!"

Amelia replies, "That's a super idea! But if you get back before me, please don't lock me out."

❧ Friday January 24

Justin is an artist – a modern artist. Recently he married Hilary. Hilary's mother called round to see them both a few weeks after the honeymoon.

"How are things?" she enquired.

"Wonderful," answered Hilary. "Justin paints and I cook. Then we guess what he's painted and what I've cooked."

❧ Saturday January 25

"What do you love most about me?" Julian asks his wife. "Is it my good looks or my superior intellect?"

His wife replies, "What I love about you most is your extraordinary sense of humour."

❧ Sunday January 26

What is a bargain? Something you don't need at a price you can't ignore.

❧ Monday January 27

Why is it that if you tell the boss you were late for work because you had a flat tyre, the very next morning you will have a flat tyre?

❧ Tuesday January 28

Jess comes home and explains to her husband that there seems to be a problem with the new car.

"I think it's got water in the carburettor," she says.

"Water in the carburettor? That can't be right!" her husband exclaims, very puzzled.

Jess insists, "There is, there's definitely water in the carburettor."

"But Jess, my dear, you don't even know what a carburettor is. Where is the car? Let me have a look at it."

Jess explains, "Didn't I say? It's in the river."

❧ Wednesday January 29

We just made it to the railway station as our train was about to leave and I said to the guard at the train, "Do I have time to say goodbye to my wife?"

"That depends, sir," replied the guard. "How long have you been married?"

❧ Thursday January 30

Why is it that Dad tries to carry twelve plastic shopping bags in each hand rather than taking two trips to bring the shopping in from the car?

❧ Friday January 31

Why is it that a man who invests your money is called a broker?

"I like change, but only a bit at a time."

February

❧ Saturday February 1

They were both so excited about the wedding. Mummy and little Patricia were outside the church, watching all the wedding guests having their photographs taken. After everyone had set off to the reception, Patricia asked, "Mummy, why did the bride change her mind?"

"What do you mean, change her mind?" Mummy replied.

"Well," said Patricia, "she arrived at the church with one man and came out with a different one."

❧ Sunday February 2

Just married:

"Darling, don't expect the first few meals to be great. It takes time to find a good take-away."

❧ Monday February 3

She said she was just approaching fifty. We couldn't help wondering from which direction.

❧ Tuesday February 4

I heard Dad say to Mum, "Will you love me when I'm old, fat and ugly?"
   Mum replied, "Of course I do!"

❧ Wednesday February 5

In the Main Street Church Bulletin:

"As you know, our organist, Mr Flowers, retires next Sunday after playing our organ for forty years. After the service the choir will sing 'Break Forth Into Joy'."

❧ Thursday February 6

The world is full of willing people: some willing to work and some willing to let them.

❧ Friday February 7

Alfie sat down, stuck his tongue out of the corner of his mouth and, concentrating very hard, wrote:

"Dear Granny, I'm very sorry I forgot to send you a birthday card last week.

It would serve me right if you forgot that it's my birthday next Tuesday, the 17th of March. Love from Alfie."

❧ Saturday February 8

You know you are getting a bit older when people phone at 9 pm and ask, "Did I wake you?"

❧ Sunday February 9

Mary came home with a school report card from her teacher, who had written, "When it comes to her work, Mary stops at nothing … This is the problem."

❧ Monday February 10

The ageing process has got you in its grasp when you put in low-wattage bulbs to keep the lights low, so guests can't see the dust.

❧ Tuesday February 11

If you tell the truth, you don't have to remember anything.

❧ Wednesday February 12

Nineteenth-century four-poster bed for sale. Perfect for antique lover.

❧ Thursday February 13

Remember – you aren't learning much when your lips are moving.

❧ Friday February 14

Why is it that when you open a tin with a butterfly tin-opener the lid falls in?

"Want my pickle?"

❧ Saturday February 15

Grandpa started walking five miles a day when he took early retirement at 60. He's 97 years old now and we don't know where he is.

❧ Sunday February 16

Dinner at the manor was a little late. A guest asked the hostess to play something to entertain them. Seating herself at the piano, she played a Chopin nocturne with absolute precision.

When she was finished, the butler signalled to her that dinner was still not ready.

Turning to an elderly guest on her right she said, "Would you like a sonata before going in to dinner?"

He gave her a look of surprise and pleasure as he responded, "Why, yes, please! I had a couple on my way here, but I would very much like another."

❧ Monday February 17

We like long walks, especially when they are taken by people who annoy us.

❧ Tuesday February 18

When Mum says, "Do what you want", what she really means is, "You'll pay for the consequences later."

❧ Wednesday February 19

You might like to take up cross-country running, but, to begin with, start with a small country.

❧ Thursday February 20

In the Main Street Church Bulletin:

"Our own Theatre Players will present Shakespeare's *Hamlet* in the large hall on Friday at 7.30 pm. The congregation is invited to attend this tragedy."

❧ Friday February 21

Don't be irreplaceable. If you can't be replaced, you can't be promoted.

❧ Saturday February 22

The farmer was busy working on his tractor when a passing American tourist asked, "How much land do you have here?" The farmer replied, "About 20 acres."

"You know back home it takes me a day to drive around my ranch!" boasted the American. "Yes," said the farmer, "I once had a car like that."

❧ Sunday February 23

Misers aren't great to live with but they make good ancestors.

❧ Monday February 24

Money doesn't bring you happiness, but it helps you to look for it in more places.

❧ Tuesday February 25

Grandpa had to go up a trouser size and he observed, "Did you know that the roman numerals for 40 are 'XL'?"

❧ Wednesday February 26

Why is it that wise guys and wise men are opposites?

❧ Thursday February 27

A boy came home from school and told his mother he had been given a part in the school play.

"Wonderful," said his mother. "What part is it?" The boy said, "I play the part of the husband!" The mother scowled and said, "Go back and tell your teacher you want a speaking part."

❧ Friday February 28

I talk to myself because I like dealing with sensible people.

March

❧ Saturday March 1

Jenny came home from Sunday School and told her mother that she had learned a new song about "a cross-eyed bear named Gladly".

It took her mother a while before she realised that the song was actually the hymn "Gladly the Cross I'd Bear".

❧ Sunday March 2

Can someone tell me how the man that drives the snow plough gets to work?

❧ Monday March 3

What you need to know about golf is that bad shots come in batches of three. A fourth bad shot is the beginning of the next batch.

❧ Tuesday March 4

When Mum says "We need to talk", what she really means is "I have a complaint".

❧ Wednesday March 5

One young mum was doing her hair with heated hair tongs. "What are you doing Mummy?" asked her little daughter.

"I'm putting waves in my hair," came the reply.

The little girl was crouched on her father's lap, watching intently. Every once in a while her little fingers would slide over her father's bald head. Eventually she said, "No waves for you, Daddy – you're all beach."

❧ Thursday March 6

Why is it that a piece of wood cut to length will be too short?

২৯ Friday March 7

Grandpa explained it:

"A good politician must be able to see both sides of an issue, so he can get around it."

২৯ Saturday March 8

If you look like your passport picture, you probably need a holiday.

২৯ Sunday March 9

The teacher was instructing her young pupils in the use of the hyphen, and among other examples was the word "bird-cage".

"Now, Lewis," she said encouragingly to one of the boys, "tell me why we put a hyphen in 'bird-cage'."

"For the bird to sit on," was the surprising answer.

"You busy?"

❧ Monday March 10

Small advertisement in the newsagent's window:

"Dog seeks a good home. Not a fussy eater. Likes children."

❧ Tuesday March 11

A chauffeur worked for a wealthy woman who always took her cat with her on outings in her large limousine.

During one trip, the driver dropped her at a department store then went to the petrol station to fill up the tank. The cat stayed in the car and lay down on the top of the back seat.

The service station's attendant glanced at the unusual passenger then asked, "Sir, is that cat someone important?"

❧ Wednesday March 12

"Dad? Can you tell me how I will know if I am enlightened?"

❧ Thursday March 13

An expert is a man who has made all the mistakes which can be made, in a very narrow field.

❧ Friday March 14

Talk is cheap because supply exceeds demand.

❧ Saturday March 15

In the Main Street Church Bulletin:

"The Very Reverend Malcolm Millar, who ministered to this parish until his retirement ten years ago, spoke briefly – much to the delight of the congregation."

❧ Sunday March 16

The furniture store advertised:

"Get your new bedroom suite from us, and we will stand behind it for twelve months."

❧ Monday March 17

Hat and coat on, Mrs Small gathered her keys and said to her husband, "I'm going to town this morning."

"Shopping, dearest?" came the reply.

"No, I haven't time for that today. I'm just going to buy some things I need."

❧ Tuesday March 18

A young dad-to-be went into action and dialled 999.

"My wife is getting contractions only two minutes apart!"

"Is this her first child?"

"No – it's her husband!"

❧ Wednesday March 19

Old John was always complaining about his health:

"Hypochondria is the only disease I haven't got!"

"I want you to know. I celebrate your diversity."

ૐ Thursday March 20

A grandfather was listening to his grandchildren arguing with their parents.
When they called upon him to settle the dispute, he simply remarked, "I am not young enough to know everything."

ૐ Friday March 21

Small advertisement in our local paper:

Tired of cleaning yourself day-in, day-out? Let me do it!

ૐ Saturday March 22

Mr Smith thought he would treat himself to some new cushions for his conservatory. He looked at what they had in the shop and remarked that they seemed very expensive, to which the assistant said, "Sir, down is up!"

⋟ Sunday March 23

I decided, given my great age, that I would go to the fancy dress party as Old Father Time. But where could I get a scythe? I tried the agricultural supplier near us. The man there scratched his head and said, "Would a lawnmower do?"

⋟ Monday March 24

Why is it that you have to try on a pair of sunglasses with that plastic thing and a price tag dangling in the middle?

⋟ Tuesday March 25

The clerk at a busy hotel approached the manager:

"The painters are decorating my office this week. I don't suppose you have anywhere I could squeeze a typist for a few days?"

ᴈ Wednesday March 26

Miss Holly was a very well-liked primary school teacher who encouraged parents into the classroom at every opportunity and organised many little outings to which the whole family could come.

She got on a train at the local station one day and sitting down opposite a very elegant looking man she said brightly, "Good morning, Mr Thomson."

Evidently the gentleman did not know her and she realised her mistake.

"I am so sorry," she said, "I thought you were the father of one of my children."

ᴈ Thursday March 27

Grandpa explained it:

"A good politician is someone who stands for what he thinks the voters will fall for."

"I work outside the home, inside the home, and occasionally on top of the home."

❧ Friday March 28

Never judge a book by its movie.

❧ Saturday March 29

Whatever the game, no matter how badly you are playing, it is always possible to play worse.

❧ Sunday March 30

The label on my new top says, "Do not machine wash or tumble dry". That means I will not wash it – ever.

❧ Monday March 31

Letter from the Session Clerk in the Main Street Church Bulletin:

"Dear friends, by now you will all know that our minister is leaving us for pastures new. I therefore ask that you make a small contribution to give him a little momentum!"

"Let's try once again without the parachute."

April

❧ Tuesday April 1

The lifeguard was giving little Harry's mother a lecture, but she was hearing none of it.

"Everyone knows that all small children will take a leak in a pool when they get excited. They get caught short. That's surely why the pool is so heavily chlorinated."

"Is that right?" said the lifeguard. "The problem is your dear little boy was doing it from the high dive."

❧ Wednesday April 2

When Mum says, "You have to learn to communicate," what she really means is "Why don't you just agree with me?"

❧ Thursday April 3

Middle age is when narrowness of the waist and broadness of the mind change places.

❧ Friday April 4

Why is it that you leave a tiny paper handkerchief in a trouser pocket in the wash and the entire load comes out covered in white bits?

❧ Saturday April 5

The manager scowled at the shop assistant, who had arrived late for work again.

"You should have been here at nine o'clock!" he exclaimed.

"Why?" she quickly replied. "What happened?"

⊱ Sunday April 6

We were looking through Granny's wedding album. Grandpa looked at one of the pictures.

"I remember," he said, "your Grandma calling to me on our honeymoon. 'Breakfast will be ready if you make the toast and pour the orange juice,' she said. 'Great,' I said, 'what's for breakfast?' 'Toast and orange juice,' she said."

⊱ Monday April 7

If dogs have masters, cats must have staff.

⊱ Tuesday April 8

If you suffer from tension migraines and headaches, do exactly what it says on the bottle:

"Take two and keep away from children."

❧ Wednesday April 9

It had not been an easy afternoon for the teacher who took her pupils through the Museum of Natural History, but their enthusiastic interest in the stuffed animals and their open-eyed wonder at the prehistoric fossils amply repaid her.

"Well, boys, where have you been all afternoon?" asked the father of two of the class that evening. The answer came back with joyous promptness. "Oh, Dad! Teacher took us to a dead zoo."

❧ Thursday April 10

It is not a good idea to allow a child wearing Superman pyjamas to sleep in the top bunk.

❧ Friday April 11

Why is it that people will believe anything if you whisper it to them?

⅔ Saturday April 12

A puddle is a small body of water which attracts other small bodies wearing dry shoes and socks into it.

⅔ Sunday April 13

Even if you are on the right track, you'll get run over if you just sit there.

⅔ Monday April 14

Why is it that one careless tossed match can start a forest fire, but it takes a whole box to start a campfire?

⅔ Tuesday April 15

The reason a dog has so many friends is that he wags his tail instead of his tongue.

⅔ Wednesday April 16

All generalisations are bad.

❧ Thursday April 17

Mum was making pancakes for her two little boys, Peter and James. As usual, an argument started about which of them was going to get the first pancake.

Mum kept calm and chose her moment.

"Remember what you were talking about at Sunday School?" she said. "If Jesus was here he wouldn't argue. He would say, 'I will wait. Let my brother have the first pancake.'"

There was silence for a moment.

Mum was pleased at having made her point, but then Peter turned to James and said, "James – your turn to be Jesus."

❧ Friday April 18

Note from the Church Magazine:

"Miss Katherine May sang 'I will not pass this way again', giving obvious pleasure to the congregation."

"I say we give him some space
until he puts back the happy face flag."

❧ Saturday April 19

The reason you give a child a middle name is so he can tell when he's really, really in trouble.

❧ Sunday April 20

We never really grow up, we just learn how to act in public.

❧ Monday April 21

Tommy's aunt looked at him in a kindly manner, "Won't you have another piece of cake, Tommy?"

Tommy was on a rare visit with his mother. "No, thank you," he mumbled.

"You seem to be suffering from a loss of appetite," said his aunt.

"Not really, Auntie, it isn't a loss of appetite. What I'm suffering from is politeness."

?❧ Tuesday April 22

The local paper carried this small advertisement:

"Low Self-Esteem Support Group will meet Thursday at 7 sharp. Please use the back door."

?❧ Wednesday April 23

One good turn gets the duvet.

?❧ Thursday April 24

At school, Peter was asked this question in physics, "What is the difference between lightning and electricity?"

Peter paused, thought and said, "Well, you don't have to pay for lightning."

?❧ Friday April 25

Why do "oversee" and "overlook" mean completely different things?

❧ Saturday April 26

"I had a tricky moment last night," said one husband to another.

"What happened?"

"Well, I was home really late, and my wife heard me and said, 'Is that you? What time is it?' and I called, 'Only twelve o'clock.' And just then that blooming cuckoo clock of ours cuckooed three times."

"What did you do?"

"I just had to stand there and cuckoo another nine times."

❧ Sunday April 27

From the national press:

"Before the present government came to power, we were on the edge of an economic cliff. Since then we've taken a great leap forward."

❧ Monday April 28

The ferry-dock was crowded with weary home-goers when through the crowd rushed a man – hot, excited, with a suitcase in each hand and a pack on his back.

He sprinted down the pier, his eyes fixed on a ferryboat only two or three feet out from the pier. He paused for but an instant and then, cheered on by the amused crowd, he made a flying leap across the intervening stretch of water and landed safely on the deck. A man happened to be standing on the exact spot on which he landed, and they both went down with a resounding crash.

When the arriving man had somewhat recovered his breath he apologised. "I hope I didn't hurt you," he said. "I am really sorry. But at least I caught the boat!"

"But," said the other man, "the boat was coming in!"

ᚦ Tuesday April 29

If your dog is fat, you aren't getting enough exercise.

ᚦ Wednesday April 30

A young lady who had returned from a tour through Italy with her father informed a friend that her father liked all the Italian cities, but most of all he loved Venice.

"Ah, Venice!" said the friend. "I can understand that your father would like Venice with its gondolas, St. Mark's and Titian."

"Oh, no," the young lady interrupted, "it wasn't that. He liked it because he could sit in the hotel and fish from the window."

"Yesterday I finally learned self-acceptance.
Today the boss told me to change."

May

❧ Thursday May 1

"Dad? Why do they call where we live 'apartments' when they are all stuck together?"

❧ Friday May 2

A car repair service advertised in the local paper:

"Free pick-up and delivery. Try us once, you'll never go anywhere again."

❧ Saturday May 3

Mary was being a bit superior, having had a good mark in her English essay. She explained, "I used to use clichés all the time but now I avoid them like the plague."

❧ Sunday May 4

Why is it that everyone wants a bus service to their door, but no one wants a bus service in their street?

❧ Monday May 5

Everyone makes mistakes. The trick is to make them when nobody is looking.

❧ Tuesday May 6

In the Main Street Church Bulletin:

"The Thursday Faith Healing Group meeting is postponed due to the Minister's illness."

❧ Wednesday May 7

If God had meant us to travel economy class, he would have made us narrower.

❧ Thursday May 8

On the label of a waterproofing spray:

"Regardless of what your coat is made of, this spray will make it 100% repellent."

❧ Friday May 9

An expert is someone who knows more and more about less and less until he knows everything about nothing.

❧ Saturday May 10

We heard screams coming from little Penny's room and rushed upstairs to find her standing on a chair pointing at the tiniest spider you have ever seen.

"Don't be silly, it's just a baby spider," said Dad.

Penny wailed even more. "Well that means that there will be a big mummy and a daddy around here somewhere!"

❧ Sunday May 11

I used to have a handle on life, then it broke.

❧ Monday May 12

A bus station is where a bus stops. A train station is where a train stops. My desk is a work station …

❧ Tuesday May 13

Why is it that when I am dieting, the days seem longer and the meals seem shorter?

❧ Wednesday May 14

Education is what you get from reading the small print on the instructions. Experience is what you get from not reading it.

"You said this was 'casual' dress day.
Well, this is the only casual dress I own.
All my other dresses are formal."

❧ Thursday May 15

Research is what I do when I don't know what I am doing.

❧ Friday May 16

If you drop buttered toast onto the floor, the probability of it landing, melted, dripping and butter-side down, is directly proportional to the cost of the floor covering it lands on.

❧ Saturday May 17

If you keep your head when all about you are losing theirs, you probably don't understand the problem.

❧ Sunday May 18

If your uninvited visitors are outstaying their welcome, all you need to do is get out the photographs from your last holiday.

❧ Monday May 19

"Dad? Who discovered that you can eat frog's legs?"

❧ Tuesday May 20

The Twins pestered their mum all day to take them to the movies until she could put up with it no more, saying, "The decision is maybe and that's final!"

❧ Wednesday May 21

My inferiority complex isn't as good as yours.

❧ Thursday May 22

There's a sign on the antique shop in the village:

"Come and buy what your Grandma threw away."

❧ Friday May 23

Why is it that sometimes the only decent things on TV are the vase and the flowers?

❧ Saturday May 24

Why is it called "rush hour"? That's the very time when the traffic doesn't go anywhere.

❧ Sunday May 25

Why is it that regardless of whether it is in a supermarket or at passport control, the other queue always moves faster?

❧ Monday May 26

The shortest measure of time is the period between the traffic light turning green and the white van man behind you blowing his horn.

ঌ Tuesday May 27

As an anniversary treat we went to a five-star hotel for a weekend break. The room was fabulous. The toiletries were lovely, except that Harold had to complain about the soap. It just didn't work! He took it to the front desk and the receptionist apologised profusely and went to get another bar, which he brought back on a small silver tray.

Then, in front of Harold's eyes, he removed the tight shrink-wrap from the soap and said, "I think you will find this one works, sir!"

ঌ Wednesday May 28

There was an article in the paper about the dangers of medication which Granny read out loud to us. Then she commented, "These pills I take can't be habit-forming. I've been taking them for years."

"Please don't ask me to remind you to
do anything else in a while."

❧ Thursday May 29

Little Lucy had asked Grandpa why he had no hair. He explained that he was bald.

Lucy thought, felt his head, and then said, "There's one thing about being bald – it's neat."

❧ Friday May 30

Why is it that kids always make complicated snacks just after I have cleaned the kitchen?

❧ Saturday May 31

Jess reckoned the best place to meet a young single man was at the laundrette. She believed that the young men who used a launderette usually had jobs and cared about their appearance, and she says you can tell a lot about a man by looking at his laundry.

June

❧ Sunday June 1

They think I'm paranoid. They all talk about it behind my back.

❧ Monday June 2

The ageing process has got you in its grasp when you start noticing that they are remaking your favourite films in colour.

❧ Tuesday June 3

Sitting at breakfast with my little brother, Mum, who had been thinking about going back to work part-time, said, "I'm not going to be just a mother anymore. I've got a job!"

My little brother burst into tears and cried, "Will we have to go to an orphanage?"

"Yes, I did hire a seven-year-old. He's the only person I know who knows anything about social networking."

❧ Wednesday June 4

Why is it that work expands to fit the time available for it to be completed?

❧ Thursday June 5

One spring afternoon, I came home to find two little girls on the steps of my flat.

Both were crying hard, shedding big tears. Thinking they might be hurt, I quickly went over to them.

"Are you all right?" I asked. Still sobbing, one held up her doll. "My baby's arm came off," she said.

I took the doll and its disjointed arm. After a little effort and luck, the doll was again whole.

"Thank you," came a whisper.

Next, looking into the tearful eyes of her friend, I asked, "And what's the matter with you, young lady?"

She wiped her cheeks. "I was helping her cry," she said.

❧ Friday June 6

Why is it that bills come by post much faster than cheques?

❧ Saturday June 7

Conscience is what hurts when everything else feels great.

❧ Sunday June 8

My Auntie Kath lives in a flat above an elderly lady who lives on her own, but she hadn't seen her around for a day or so.

Auntie called to her son, "Go and find out how old Mrs Davis is."

So six-year-old Andrew went down and rang Mrs Davis's doorbell.

"So how is she?" asked Auntie when Andrew returned.

"She said to say it's none of your business how old she is."

❧ Monday June 9

It's such a pity that the very people who know how to run the country properly are too busy driving taxis, cutting hair and serving beer.

❧ Tuesday June 10

Why is it that nothing ever turns out like it looks on the seed packet?

❧ Wednesday June 11

Knowledge is knowing a tomato is a fruit. Wisdom is not putting a tomato in a fruit salad.

❧ Thursday June 12

You can tell that your son is growing up when he looks at a girl the way he used to look at chocolate pudding.

"There was some misunderstanding about the term 'island'."

❧ Friday June 13

My grandson is five years old. I told him he was growing up too fast and needed to slow down.

"It isn't my fault, Grandad," he replied. "It's Mum's fault. She keeps giving me birthday parties."

❧ Saturday June 14

Why is it that when Elsie, Mary, Katie and Jenny go out they will call each other Elsie, Mary, Katie and Jenny, but if Mike, John, Harry and Tom go out, they will high-five each other and say, "Hey – Big Man, Dodger, Rhino and Shortie"?

❧ Sunday June 15

Evening news is where they begin with "Good Evening" and then proceed to tell you why it isn't.

"You should check your email more often, Smythe. I fired you over three weeks ago."

❧ Monday June 16

When all else fails, read the instructions.

❧ Tuesday June 17

Artificial intelligence is no match for natural stupidity.

❧ Wednesday June 18

A synonym is a word you use if you can't spell the other one.

❧ Thursday June 19

I was talking to my four-year-old grandson on the phone but I couldn't make out all he was saying so I kept saying, "Pardon?"

Finally, exasperated, he said, "Grandpa, you're not listening loud enough!"

❧ Friday June 20

A balanced diet is an éclair in each hand.

❧ Saturday June 21

Why is it that a woman marries a man on the basis that he will change, but he doesn't, and a man marries a woman on the basis that she won't change, yet she does.

❧ Sunday June 22

From the court:

"Please state your name."
"Victoria Darling Purnell."
"And your marital status?"
"Fair."

❧ Monday June 23

At exactly what point does a child who is afraid of the dark change into a teenager who wants to stay out all night?

❧ Tuesday June 24

"Remember son," said Dad, "women always have the last word in an argument. Anything you add after that is the start of a new argument."

❧ Wednesday June 25

Touring a large National Trust country house, young Ian asked his dad, "Why have they got deer heads on their walls?"

His dad replied, "Because they are beautiful and people are proud of them."

A few minutes later, Ian said "Dad, you said that Mum is beautiful, but we only have photographs of her on our wall."

❧ Thursday June 26

"Now look here! I don't have an attitude problem – you have a perception problem."

❧ Friday June 27

"Have you been in the car with Grandpa lately? Have you noticed that anyone going slower than him is an idiot, and anyone going faster than him is a maniac?"

❧ Saturday June 28

In the TV advertisement they show that you can use their soap powder to get bloodstains out of shirts. That made me think maybe you have problems other than just your laundry.

❧ Sunday June 29

Why is it that when they eventually open another check-out lane at the supermarket to relieve the queue pressure, everybody behind you gets there first?

"I told you the inflatable furniture was a mistake."

❧ Monday June 30

A thief broke into a mansion early the other morning and found himself in the music-room. Hearing footsteps approaching, he took refuge behind a screen.

From eight to nine o'clock the eldest daughter had a singing lesson. From nine to ten o'clock the second daughter took a piano lesson. From ten to eleven o'clock the eldest son had a violin lesson. From eleven to twelve o'clock the other son had a lesson on the flute.

At twelve fifteen all the brothers and sisters assembled and studied an ear-splitting piece for voice, piano, violin and flute.

The thief staggered out from behind the screen at twelve forty-five, and, falling at their feet, cried, "For Heaven's sake, have me arrested!"

July

❧ Tuesday July 1

When everything's coming your way, you're in the wrong lane.

❧ Wednesday July 2

You can fool most of the people some of the time, and some of the people most of the time, but you can't fool your mother.

❧ Thursday July 3

Long ago when people cursed and beat the ground with sticks, it was called witchcraft. Today, it's called golf.

❧ Friday July 4

The trouble with being punctual is that no one is there to appreciate it.

❧ Saturday July 5

Why is it that the more people I meet, the more I like my dog?

❧ Sunday July 6

By the time a woman realises that maybe her mother was right, she usually has a daughter who thinks she's wrong.

❧ Monday July 7

Everyone is entitled to be stupid, but some abuse the privilege.

❧ Tuesday July 8

Dad took Charlie to get his haircut. Charlie sat high up on the chair and the hairdresser said, "What's it to be today, young sir?"

"I'd like it like Daddy's with a big hole on the top."

"My horse needs exercise, and I need a company vehicle … that's when it dawned on me."

❧ Wednesday July 9
A true friend walks in when the rest of the world walks out.

❧ Thursday July 10
A friend is one who knows all about you and likes you anyway.

❧ Friday July 11
When dieting, if you eat something and no one sees you eat it then it has no calories.

❧ Saturday July 12
Nothing makes a person more productive than the last minute.

❧ Sunday July 13
The ageing process has got you in its grasp if you never get the urge to throw a snowball or build a sandcastle.

"Who knows how far up we are?
Raise your hands."

❧ Monday July 14

Our days are happier when we give people a bit of our heart rather than a piece of our mind.

❧ Tuesday July 15

One summer evening, I was sitting out on the porch with my granddaughter and telling her about when I was a girl her age. "We had a treehouse, and we went horse-riding, we had our own swing, we went swimming and sailing at the lake, and we had apples and pears from the orchard." My granddaughter was open-mouthed and said "Oh, Granny, I wish I'd met you sooner!"

❧ Wednesday July 16

Why is it that a child always grows fastest the month after you've just bought a whole new school uniform?

"Now where was I?"

⸎ Thursday July 17

Time is a great healer, but it's a terrible beautician.

⸎ Friday July 18

Old Mr Marple was standing in the baker's shop, peering at the wonderful display of cakes and pastries.

The baker picked up his tongs and a bag and asked the old man, "What would you like?"

There was a pause, then he replied, "I'd like that chocolate-covered, cream-filled éclair, that strawberry tart and that pecan pie – but I'll take that oat-bran roll."

⸎ Saturday July 19

"Dad, where are the Alps?"

"If you would do what I tell you and put your stuff away properly, you'd know where to find them!"

❧ Sunday July 20

Little James was really quite unwell but he refused to take the awful tasting medicine the doctor had prescribed. His mother gave up.

"Oh, James," she said, "you won't get better if you don't take your medicine."

Her face fell and she was just about at the end of her tether. But a little voice spoke up from the bed, "Don't worry, Mum. Dad'll be home soon and he'll make me take it."

❧ Monday July 21

Alan came with us to church yesterday for the first time. He watched as the collection plate was passed round and whispered, "Don't pay for me. I'm under five."

❧ Tuesday July 22

All of us could take a lesson from the weather. It pays no attention to criticism.

"Last guy up blows out the candles."

❧ Wednesday July 23

Grandpa lives on his own. He always has some get well cards on the table, so that if any visitors come they'll think he's not been so well and hasn't been able to do the dusting.

❧ Thursday July 24

You know you are getting on a bit when several items in your shopping trolley say "for fast relief".

❧ Friday July 25

Believe half of what you see and nothing of what you hear.

❧ Saturday July 26

Why is it that the mother with the crying baby always sits opposite you on the train?

❦ Sunday July 27

Experience is something you don't get until just after you need it.

❦ Monday July 28

I was in the queue at the computer games counter when the woman in front said to the assistant, "I need a game that will keep my six year old quiet but it's got to be simple enough that my husband can understand it."

❦ Tuesday July 29

Always use tasteful words. You never know when you might have to eat them.

❦ Wednesday July 30

People have one thing in common. They're all different.

"Profits are down, competition is up
and someone's sticking gum under the chairs!"

❧ Thursday July 31

A motorcyclist skidded on ice and man and machine ended up at the side of the road.

A small crowd gathered and a young woman went into action, only to be pushed to one side by an older man who announced, "Get out of my way – I'm a trained first aider!"

The young woman did so, watched for a moment, then said, "When you get to the bit where you have stabilised the patient and then need to call a doctor – I'm right here."

August

❧ Friday August 1

The optician pointed at the chart on the wall and said, "Cover your left eye and read out the top line."

The patient read it letter-perfect.

"Very good. Now cover your right eye."

Same again – no problem.

"Now both …"

There was silence. The optician looked round and saw the patient with both eyes covered.

❧ Saturday August 2

Whoever said nothing is impossible never tried to slam a revolving door.

❧ Sunday August 3

How long a minute feels like depends on which side of the toilet door you're on.

❧ Monday August 4

My mind works like lightning. One flash and it is gone.

❧ Tuesday August 5

I was sitting watching my mother preparing the Sunday roast. She cut off the ends, laid on the herbs and seasoning and put it in the roasting tin. I asked her why she cut off the ends.

"I do that," she said, "because that's what Granny used to do."

I went through to the sitting room and asked Granny the same question. She said the same thing. After lunch we visited Great Grandpa and I asked him why Great Granny cut off the ends of the beef.

"Well," he replied, "I remember we only had a small roasting tin so you had to cut the ends off the roast to get it into the tin."

"They squared the wagons! Can they *do* that?"

❧ Wednesday August 6

You can't have everything. Where would you put it?

❧ Thursday August 7

Granny was mortified! Grandpa brought home in a police car – with all the neighbours watching. The policeman explained that they'd found him feeding the ducks at the pond and he'd said he couldn't remember the way home.

Once the police were gone, Granny rounded on him. "Why would you tell them that? You know fine well the way home!"

"I know I do," came the reply, "but my feet hurt and there wasn't a bus stop nearby."

❧ Friday August 8

Why is it that the garden tool you want is always at the very back of the shed?

❧ Saturday August 9

We promised Toby that when he was fifteen we would convert our basement to give him a bit more space, and move his room from upstairs.

What we hadn't anticipated was how much easier it would be to get him up in the morning. Instead of repeatedly yelling up the stairs, all I need to do now is switch the basement light on and off.

This morning he didn't appear as usual, so I switched the light on and off several times and heard, "All right, all right – there's no need to shout!"

❧ Sunday August 10

"Dad? Who tastes the cat food when it says 'new great flavour'?"

❧ Monday August 11

"Dad? What's dust?"
"Oh – it's just mud without the juice."

❧ Tuesday August 12

At our golf club in June we have a challenge match with the over 60s playing the under 40s.

At the tricky tenth hole, a dog-leg par 6 round a clump of very tall pine trees, the senior player I was challenging said, "When I was your age, I would have hit the ball clean over these pine trees and gone for a birdie."

That was definitely a challenge.

So I hit the ball, it flew, hit the top of the trees and fell back into a bunker.

The senior prepared to play his shot and said, "Of course, when I was your age these pine trees were only ten feet tall."

❧ Wednesday August 13

Life is a struggle punctuated by disappointments and embarrassments, but if you persevere you will find a hairdresser you like.

❧ Thursday August 14

I had my granddaughter to stay in the summer. We decided to make a patchwork cushion and I showed her how to use the sewing machine.

She watched carefully as I changed the needle, threaded the machine and adjusted everything, then said, "Granny, how come you can do all that but you can't work my laptop?"

❧ Friday August 15

Have you noticed at the golf course that everyone replaces their divot after making a perfect approach shot?

❧ Saturday August 16

Why is it that on long-haul flights the only passengers that get up repeatedly to go to the toilet have window seats?

Sunday August 17

The Bowling Club Committee? It might keep minutes but it wastes hours.

Monday August 18

Just when I was getting used to yesterday, along came today.

Tuesday August 19

Why is it that you simply hang something in your wardrobe for a month or two and it shrinks a size?

Wednesday August 20

On the golf course, if you think your drive might carry to the green before the match ahead of you has putted out, you can either carry on or wait till they are watching and duff your drive altogether.

❧ Thursday August 21

A Scottish midge is an insect that makes you like flies better.

❧ Friday August 22

Completing my passport application, in the section that says "In case of an emergency, notify", I put "doctor".

❧ Saturday August 23

Jack was in trouble. He tried to explain to his dad why he had decided to steal a bike. He told his dad that he had asked God for a bike but God had not responded. He had then asked his mum why God hadn't given him the bike he had asked for, and she told him that that wasn't how God worked. So, unable to wait any longer, he had decided to steal a bike and ask God for forgiveness instead.

❧ Sunday August 24

If I agreed with you, then we would both be wrong.

❧ Monday August 25

It was the school outing to the zoo. The young teacher had an interesting way of engaging her charges. "Penguins are so smart," she said, "that within a few weeks of captivity, they can train people to stand beside the pool and throw them fish three times a day."

❧ Tuesday August 26

When I left school, I thought I wanted a career. It turns out I just wanted a salary.

❧ Wednesday August 27

Why is it that opportunity often knocks at the least opportune moment?

"Aren't you glad we had this meeting
to resolve our conflict?"

❧ Thursday August 28

Why is it that the need to scratch an itch is inversely proportional to the ability to reach it?

❧ Friday August 29

When she got married she got a new name and a dress.

❧ Saturday August 30

Grandpa looked up from the article he was reading in his paper and said, "With all these electronic phones and gadgets, the calendar's days are numbered."

❧ Sunday August 31

Three fifths of all people do not understand fractions.

September

❧ Monday September 1

After all is said and done, more is said than done.

❧ Tuesday September 2

Let all bad spellers of the world untie!

❧ Wednesday September 3

Always check the small print. Ever had that sinking feeling on Christmas Day when you read "Batteries not included."?

❧ Thursday September 4

Why is it that the gas service engineer will never have seen a boiler quite like yours before?

"Needs oregano."

✿ Friday September 5

"Dad? Why is the alphabet in that order? Is it because of that song?"

✿ Saturday September 6

Patricia was saying her prayers. She started, "Dear Harold …"

Mum interrupted gently and said, "Pat, why are you calling God 'Harold'?"

Patricia thought for a moment. "But that's what we say in Sunday School, 'Harold be thy name'."

✿ Sunday September 7

There was a sign up at our local garage that said, "Fix and service your own car here – use our facilities." I said to the mechanic, "Are you not doing yourself out of a job?"

"Not really," he replied. "We make more money on repairs if we let people try to fix their cars themselves first."

ॐ Monday September 8

Molly from the new baby-sitting service seemed in command. The boys were dispatched to bed whilst she settled down for a night of magazines and TV.

One child did repeatedly creep down the stairs, but Molly yelled at him and sent him back upstairs to bed.

A while later the doorbell rang. It was the next-door neighbour. "I'm Mrs Taylor," she said. "Is my son here?"

"No," said Molly.

But just then came a little voice, "I'm here, but she won't let me out!"

ॐ Tuesday September 9

I started out with nothing and still have most of it left.

ॐ Wednesday September 10

Why is it that weeds grow at precisely the rate you pull them out?

❧ Thursday September 11

Why is it that dentists are incapable of asking questions that require a simple yes or no answer?

❧ Friday September 12

Harry was sent home early from his friend Barry's house and when quizzed about why, he confessed to having broken a vase when they were playing indoor cricket in the hall.

"But it's OK," he said, "you don't need to buy another vase. Barry's mother said it was irreplaceable."

❧ Saturday September 13

"Mum says you dodged school today to play football," accused Dad angrily. "What have you got to say for yourself?"

"No, I did not, and I have five fish to prove it!"

"Sure I can fix that hole ...
or we could make it a door to the porch."

❧ Sunday September 14

We are born naked, wet and hungry. Then things just get worse.

❧ Monday September 15

Lead me not into temptation, I can find it all by myself.

❧ Tuesday September 16

It's not hard to meet expenses. You'll find them everywhere.

❧ Wednesday September 17

Have you had that experience where you have put clothes away joking that you'll wait till they come back in style – and they just have?

❧ Thursday September 18

Mary and Betty did their shopping together. Both preferred to shop every day and buy just a few things so they weren't so heavy to carry.

"You can always tell the people that can't count up to ten," remarked Betty loudly.

"Yes," agreed Mary, even more loudly. "They're always in front of us at the express checkout!"

❧ Friday September 19

The primary class had an outing to the local Fire Station as part of their Industry In The Community programme.

They all wore firemen's hats and listened as the guide gave a fire safety talk. He held up a smoke detector and asked, "Who can tell me what this is?"

Little Jenny put her hand up. "It's to tell Mummy when tea is ready!"

❧ Saturday September 20

Sixty-three per cent of all statistics are worthless.

❧ Sunday September 21

The baker's shop was about to close, when in rushed an angry woman.

"I sent my son here this morning to get one of your 2-kg bags of doughnuts, and I weighed them and there's only 1.5 kgs. You need to check your scales and not take advantage of children doing errands."

The baker put bag after bag on the scales and declared, "Each of them weighs 2 kgs exactly. Madam, I suggest you weigh your son."

❧ Monday September 22

Why is it that when the train you are on is late, the train you want to transfer to is on time?

❧ Tuesday September 23

I was a police-dog handler for twenty years. One afternoon when I got back to the Police Station, my dog, Honour, was barking in the back of the van.

A small boy was looking at me. "Have you got a dog in there?" he enquired, peering in the back window.

"Yes, I have," I confirmed.

"Wow – what did you catch him doing?" asked the boy.

❧ Wednesday September 24

"Dad? If all the rivers flow into the oceans and the streams flow into the oceans, why is the sea never full up?"

❧ Thursday September 25

Isn't it frustrating, that when you know all the answers, nobody asks you the questions?

"Any jobs on the other side?"

❧ Friday September 26

Bath time for little Tommy! Even worse, Mum was washing his hair!

She said to him, "Haircut for you, young man – your hair seems to grow so fast!"

Tommy, from beneath the bubbles, replied, "Well maybe you shouldn't water it so much."

❧ Saturday September 27

Just as Timmy was getting tucked-up at bedtime after his story, a violent thunderstorm started. Mummy said goodnight as she turned off the light, but Timmy said, "Mummy I'm scared of the thunder – will you come and sleep in my bed tonight please?"

Mummy said, "Don't be scared – I'll be sleeping with Daddy just in the next room!"

Timmy pulled the covers over his head and said, "He's just a big sissy!"

✺ Sunday September 28

What was the best thing before sliced bread was invented?

✺ Monday September 29

A Freudian slip is when you say one thing but mean your mother.

✺ Tuesday September 30

The university professor found a student waiting for her outside her office.

"You gave me an F grade for this assignment. I don't deserve an F," he protested.

The professor paused and replied, "I agree, but, sadly, it is the lowest grade the faculty will allow me to award."

"How sweet is your boss? When he heard you were sick, he took the time to bring your work to you.

October

❧ Wednesday October 1

"Rodney," said the teacher, "make up a sentence about a swimming lifeguard and write it on the blackboard."

Rodney took the chalk and wrote the following sentence: "The lifeguard came out of the pool pregnant."

The class laughed and the teacher corrected the boy, saying, "Don't you know what 'pregnant' means?"

"Yes," said Rodney with complete confidence, "it means carrying a child."

❧ Thursday October 2

Our next-door-neighbour asked if he could borrow our lawnmower. Dad said he could, as long as he didn't take it out of our garden.

❧ Friday October 3

The children were busy drawing posters of their favourite Bible stories. Trevor had drawn a jumbo jet with four people. As the Sunday school teacher went round the children she came to Trevor. "It's the flight into Egypt," announced Trevor, pointing, "Mary, Joseph and the Baby Jesus."

"But who's the fourth person?" enquired the teacher.

"That's Pontius-the-Pilot," confirmed Trevor.

❧ Saturday October 4

It was the day after Parents' Night at the junior school. Philip seemed quieter than usual. His teacher sat beside him and asked if he was feeling all right.

Philip thought, sighed, then whispered, "I don't want to frighten you, but Dad says if I don't get better marks, someone is getting into real trouble!"

❧ Sunday October 5

I took Phoebe with me after nursery school to make Grandma a cup of tea. Poor Grandma wasn't at all well.

We enjoyed our tea but I noticed that Phoebe was staring at Grandma's false teeth soaking in a glass by her bed. I rapidly tried to distract Phoebe, anticipating a remark or question, but I was too late. "Grandma," she said, "have you heard about the Tooth Fairy?"

❧ Monday October 6

Why is it that the lift in our office stops at every floor and no one gets on?

❧ Tuesday October 7

The main reason for holding a children's party is to remind yourself that there are children more badly behaved than your own.

"You get extra points for keeping
your eyes on the ball."

❧ Wednesday October 8

I bought a delicious-looking cream cake at the supermarket. Why is it that they print "Keep flat, do not turn upside down" on the base of the box?

❧ Thursday October 9

There was a rule at the Church that any gifts given to the minister should be acknowledged in the Church Magazine.

The minister was presented with a case of cherry brandy by a grateful parishioner and, in the next magazine issue, the listing included the following, "The Manse acknowledges the gift of fruit and the spirit in which it was given."

❧ Friday October 10

Don't think that children misquote you. They just repeat word for word what you probably shouldn't have said.

❧ Saturday October 11

Why do we wash bath towels? Aren't we clean when we use them?

❧ Sunday October 12

John was just six. He climbed up on the sofa and peered at the wedding photograph on the bookcase. "Is that you and Mum?" he asked his dad.

"Yes," replied his father, "that was on our wedding day."

"What's a wedding?" asked John.

Quite some time later after his dad had done his best to explain, John nodded. "I understand. So that's when Mum came to work for us?"

❧ Monday October 13

The ageing process has really got you in its grasp when you start liking accordion music.

❧ Tuesday October 14

The health conundrum! Japanese people don't each much fat and don't suffer as many heart attacks as British or American people.

French people do eat a lot of fat but also suffer fewer heart attacks than the British or Americans.

Japanese people don't drink red wine and suffer fewer heart attacks than the British or Americans.

Italians drink a lot of red wine but suffer fewer heart attacks than the British or Americans.

So – eat and drink whatever you like. Just don't speak English!

❧ Wednesday October 15

Why is it that however pathetically bare your lawn, healthy grass will appear between the patio paving stones.

❧ Thursday October 16

Polly is an enthusiastic teacher of English and holds evening classes to help her students with punctuation – her passion.

One evening she passed around copies of a worksheet which had the following short sentence on it and asked her class to punctuate it as part of a homework assignment: "A woman without her man is nothing."

The women in the class wrote: "A woman: without her, man is nothing."

The men wrote: "A woman, without her man, is nothing."

❧ Friday October 17

A teenager with a nose ring, earrings and dyed hair habitually dressed in black jeans and a hooded sweatshirt. He confided in his friend, "I don't really like looking like this but at least my mother doesn't drag me anywhere."

❧ Saturday October 18

Donald and Wilma loved their caravan. They loved the freedom and peace and quiet. They grew tired and fed up, however, of their well-meaning fellow campers coming around to say hello and pass the time of day.

They didn't want to appear rude, so they simply put up a notice:

"Insurance Agents – ask us about our life policies".

❧ Sunday October 19

If it's true that we are here to help others, then what exactly do the "others" do?

❧ Monday October 20

We were discussing what we liked for breakfast. Grandpa didn't even look up from his paper as he said, "A boiled egg is hard to beat."

❧ Tuesday October 21

Early one summer evening, Fred, who was a very keen bird watcher, stood in his back garden and heard an owl hooting. He thought he'd give a hoot back and see what happened.

The owl hooted again – clearly in reply. This went on all summer and he made notes of the time of day and the length of his call and the response.

Fred's wife had her next-door-neighbour in for a cup of tea.

"My husband spends his evenings calling to owls," she remarked.

"That's very odd," the neighbour replied. "So does my husband."

❧ Wednesday October 22

Half the people you know are below average.

"Remember saying you'll give us a raise when 'pigs fly'? Well, it's time to pay up."

Thursday October 23

"Yes, Dad, Mum told me to be good, but she's been wrong before."

Friday October 24

A married couple were having their regular argument about who should make the coffee each morning.

The wife said, "You should do it, because you get up first, and then we don't have to wait as long to get our coffee."

The husband said, "You should do it, you are better at making it and I don't mind waiting for my coffee."

"No, you should do it," replied his wife, "and besides, it is in the Bible that the man should do the coffee." She held her Bible open and showed him at the top of several pages, that it indeed says "HEBREWS".

❧ Saturday October 25

Timmy was a small boy who banged his drum all day long and drove everyone in the house up the wall, along with the neighbours.

Everyone tried reasoning with him but without success. They even hid the drum, but the screaming and tantrums which resulted were worse than the incessant drumming.

Eventually, Grandpa was consulted.

He thought very carefully, then handed little Timmy a hammer and asked, "Timmy, I wonder what is INSIDE the drum?"

❧ Sunday October 26

The mechanic at the garage where my car was being serviced told me, "I didn't have the parts to repair your brakes, so I made your horn louder."

❧ Monday October 27

Dad plays football for the village team. He has a game today and has just realised that his dirty kit is still in the bag from the last match.

He shouted to Mum, "What setting do I use on the washing machine?"

"It depends," she replied. "What does it say on your shirt?"

He yelled back, "Burnham Rovers, Number 9."

❧ Tuesday October 28

Toby was in the Ladies' Department in the store and hesitatingly walked up to the sales assistant. He said, "I would quite like to buy my wife a very pretty scarf."

"How lovely," responded the sales assistant, trying to put the man at ease. "That will be a great surprise."

"It certainly will be," said Toby. "She's expecting a new car!"

❧ Wednesday October 29

Our neighbour bought a new, large fridge for his kitchen.

He put the old one, which was still in good working order, outside his garage with a sign on it that read:

"FREE FRIDGE – Please take it."

It sat there for a week.

Then he changed the sign to read:

"Fridge for sale, £25."

It was stolen that night.

❧ Thursday October 30

At a school in a country town some sixth formers played a leaving prank.

They let three sheep loose inside their school, each of which had a number tied round its neck. The numbers were 1, 3 and 4.

The school janitor spent the whole day looking for a sheep wearing a number 2!

"That wasn't me barking, that was me
giving a motivational speech."

৯ Friday October 31

At the Post Office in the village where we spent our holidays there was a formidable sign on the door which said, "Danger! Beware of the dog!".

Resolving to buy my postcards as quickly as possible and retreat to safety, I noticed a very elderly Golden Labrador asleep beside the counter.

"Is that the dangerous dog?" I asked.

"Yes," said the Postmistress.

"It doesn't look terribly dangerous to me!" I remarked.

"She's not – it's just that people keep tripping over her!" came the reply.

November

❧ Saturday November 1

There is a government department responsible for policy and regulations on the environment, food and rural affairs. An inspector turned up at Hill Farm.

"Random inspection," announced the pompous inspector.

"OK," said the farmer, "but don't go in that field over there."

"Now look here!" came the response, as the inspector pulled out his badge of authority, "With this badge I can go anywhere I want to!"

The farmer shrugged and watched the Inspector head straight for that field.

Not long after he could see the Inspector running for his life with a prize bull in hot pursuit. The farmer cupped his hands and shouted, "Show him your badge!"

❧ Sunday November 2

Could it be that a clear conscience is the sign of a bad memory?

❧ Monday November 3

If you can't be kind, at least have the decency to be vague.

❧ Tuesday November 4

Why is it that your lawn is always slightly bigger than your desire to mow it?

❧ Wednesday November 5

The good thing about egotists is that they don't talk about other people.

❧ Thursday November 6

What did they go back to before they invented drawing boards?

Day of the Zombie Performance Reviews

৯ Friday November 7

Young Robert and his father went for a country walk. After a while Robert asked his father, "How can that bird fly?"

Father thought and then replied, "I don't really know how to explain that."

A few minutes passed. Robert asked, "Why does that lake not overflow its banks?" Father thought and said, "I don't know."

A little further on Robert asked, "Why are the clouds white?" Father thought and said, "I don't really know."

Robert said, "Dad, do you mind my asking you all these questions?"

"Of course not, Robert. If you don't ask questions ... how will you ever learn anything!"

৯ Saturday November 8

Nothing shatters enthusiasm like a small admission fee.

❧ Sunday November 9

Remember! The only way to guarantee rain, is to give your lawn a good watering with the hose.

❧ Monday November 10

Poor Roger. His family tried to be so encouraging as he had just taken up violin lessons. His father was trying to read a book and ignore the screeching, but Dodger the dog was lying in his basket, and every time Roger attacked the strings with his bow, the dog began to howl loudly.

Father could take it no longer! He threw his book to the floor and exclaimed, "For goodness' sake Roger – can't you play something the dog doesn't know?"

❧ Tuesday November 11

Sometimes the best helping hand you can give is a good, firm push.

❧ Wednesday November 12

I was manning the helpline at the computer store but I couldn't solve this one!

The caller said his new printer wouldn't print yellow. The other colours were fine – just the yellow didn't print. We tried everything in the troubleshooting manual.

I was just explaining how it should be sent back when the caller said "Should I try white paper instead of this yellow paper?"

❧ Thursday November 13

Tact is the art of making a point without making an enemy.

❧ Friday November 14

Money talks ... but all mine ever seems to say is goodbye!

"Yes, I live on the 9th floor, but I am unaware
of any howling sounds at night."

❧ Saturday November 15

My brother lost a contact lens in the back garden and after a lengthy search came in, sat down, and admitted defeat.

Father took up the challenge and was back within ten minutes with the lost lens in his hand.

"Wow! How did you do that?" my brother said in amazement.

"We weren't looking for the same thing," came the reply. "You were looking for a small circle of plastic. I was looking for £100."

❧ Sunday November 16

"If" is a little word with a big meaning.

❧ Monday November 17

Never resent growing old – so many are denied the privilege.

❧ Tuesday November 18

Why is it that success always happens when no one is looking, yet failure is always in full view of everyone?

❧ Wednesday November 19

We wondered why my brother wanted the whole family to have dinner together.

"I wanted to say that I've just been to see about joining the Army," he announced.

Grandma gasped, Dad spluttered his wine, and his brothers started laughing, as Johnnie wasn't exactly the outdoors type. "You?" they commented, "on an assault course?" And this was followed by more unkind laughter.

Mother was incredibly calm and just carried on eating, until finally she said, "Johnnie, do you really think you can make your own bed every morning?"

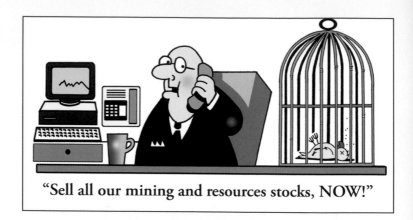

"Sell all our mining and resources stocks, NOW!"

❧ Thursday November 20

Whenever the phone rings after 9 pm, my wife turns to me and says, "Who's that phoning at this time of night?"

I always reply "I don't know. If we knew that we wouldn't need the phone, would we?"

❧ Friday November 21

Beryl came into the kitchen to find her husband swishing the air with a fly swatter. "What are you doing Fred?"

"Swatting flies," answered Fred.

"Did you get any?" asked Beryl.

"Yes, so far, two males and two females," he replied.

"Don't be ridiculous – how can you tell them apart?"

Fred paused. "Two were on the beer can, two were on the phone."

❧ Saturday November 22

The Army was on manoeuvres. A captain was driving his jeep down a country lane when he came across a staff car with a flag on the front, stuck in the mud with an angry general in the driver's seat.

"Your car stuck, sir?" asked the captain, saluting as he approached.

"Nope," yelled the general, handing him the keys, "yours is."

❧ Sunday November 23

Why is it that just after you have put air in your tyre, you have to struggle to take the thing off and it lets a whole lot of air escape?

❧ Monday November 24

How do you stop your dog from digging in the garden? Don't let the dog see you digging!

❧ Tuesday November 25

When the chicken had finished roasting for friends arriving for dinner, I left it to rest. Ceilidh, my Black Labrador, thought she should check it was properly cooked.

When I came back into the kitchen there was no trace of it, not even the bones. Lesson learned!

❧ Wednesday November 26

A pharmacist was recently asked by one of his customers, "What does one twice a day mean?"

"It means 'one twice a day'."

"What if I were to take two once a day, is that the same?"

❧ Thursday November 27

Hard work doesn't harm anyone, but I do not want to take any chances.

❧ Friday November 28

When my niece was still a baby, her socks kept going missing. We found them a couple of days later when taking the dog for a walk.

❧ Saturday November 29

Why is it that when you blow in a dog's face he gets mad at you, but when you take him in a car he sticks his head out the window?

❧ Sunday November 30

The ageing process has really got you in its grasp when it takes several attempts to negotiate a speed bump.

December

❧ Monday December 1

Have you tried the garlic diet? You don't lose any weight, but from a distance your friends swear you look thinner.

❧ Tuesday December 2

The garden weeding rule:

"To check if you are removing a weed or a plant, just pull on it. If it comes out easily, it is a valuable plant."

❧ Wednesday December 3

Snow closed the roads and schools for a week. When the school re-opened the teacher asked what the class had done in that time. Mary put her hand up and said, "Prayed for more snow, Miss!"

"Remember, we don't beg.
We make a list."

❧ Thursday December 4

To raise money for new goalposts, the village football team decided that this Christmas they would go carol singing round the houses. It was decided that they would have to have a practice, and they all met at the park and got started.

The captain was doing his best to teach the unlikely choristers. "Right then," he said, "that's the first verse of 'Good King Wenceslas'. What comes next?"

A small boy who had been watching the proceedings with interest piped up, "Ring the bell and watch out for the dog!"

❧ Friday December 5

Why is it that we spend the first twelve months of our children's lives encouraging and willing them to walk and talk, then the next twenty years telling them to sit down and shut up?

"Smile and pretend we're the family
in the Christmas letter I'm sending."

֎ Saturday December 6

Young Rupert had just passed his driving test. The whole family got into the car for a drive. Dad sat right behind the new driver.

"Don't you want to sit up front Dad?"

"No, Son," replied Dad, "I'm going to sit here and kick the back of your seat as you drive, just like you've been doing all these years."

֎ Sunday December 7

My dad went to the local florist and said, "I'd like some flowers please."

"Of course, sir," said the florist. "What would you like?"

Dad paused and said, "Well I'm not really sure, I, uh, er ..."

"Maybe I can help. What exactly is it that you have done?"

"Have you done any shopping yet?"

❧ Monday December 8

What is the secret to getting a 15-year-old daughter to answer a straightforward question without rolling her eyes in that "Are you stupid?" way?

❧ Tuesday December 9

Can someone tell this distressed mother where I can find a supermarket that doesn't have chocolate bars and chewing gum displayed at the checkout line?

❧ Wednesday December 10

It is great being a Senior Citizen – you don't have to run anywhere.

❧ Thursday December 11

The ageing process has really got you in its grasp when you start winning at trivia games.

❧ Friday December 12

Paul nodded off to sleep at his desk in the open-plan office and snored gently. His supervisor tapped him on the shoulder.

"Oh, terribly sorry, sir," said Paul and then with a brainwave he added, "They said this might happen when I was at the Blood Donor Centre earlier."

❧ Saturday December 13

"Ah," she sighed, "for many years I've suffered from dyspepsia."

"And don't you take anything for it?" her friend asked. "You look healthy enough."

"Oh," she replied, "I haven't got indigestion, my husband has."

❧ Sunday December 14

If you have a difficult task to do, ask a lazy person. They will usually find an easier way to do it.

"We can finish decorating in an hour.
Three hours if the kids help."

"I find the V12 engine with dual overhead camshafts to be particularly compelling."

❧ Monday December 15

Sheila asks her friend, "Why is it that Brian can remember the points position of every club in the league for the last ten years, the Cub Scout's promise, the registration number of every car he has ever owned, and every goal he ever scored, by match and season, yet he forgets my birthday!"

❧ Tuesday December 16

You know it is going to be a difficult day when you turn on the TV and they are showing emergency routes out of the city.

❧ Wednesday December 17

If love is blind, why is lingerie so important?

❧ Thursday December 18

Despite the cost of living, it is still popular.

❧ Friday December 19

Dorothy, one of the elders of the community, spotted the shopkeeper sweeping outside his store and asked after his wife.

"I hope your wife is getting better. There aren't many in the town like her you know."

The shopkeeper replied "No, Miss, there aren't many that do."

❧ Saturday December 20

Young girl:
"Please, Mum says will you give me the broom you borrowed last Thursday?"
Neighbour:
"Yes, but don't forget to bring it back."

❧ Sunday December 21

Indecision is the key to flexibility.

❧ Monday December 22

A visitor to one of the islands of Scotland was getting really fed up of day after day of grey cloud and drizzling rain.

After two weeks of this he asked a youngster who was passing, "Does the weather here ever change?"

To which the youngster replied, "How would I know? I'm only ten years old."

❧ Tuesday December 23

A Sunday school teacher was surprised to hear one of the children reciting the Lord's Prayer in a slightly amended fashion:

"And lead us not into temptation, But deliver us our e-mail ..."

❧ Wednesday December 24

A difficult prospective tenant, who had been looking over yet another house shown to him by a weary estate agent, remarked, "I think, after all, a flat would probably suit us better."

"Well, sir, for myself," said the agent, "I feel a flat is so much like a prison. But then, of course, it all depends on what you're accustomed to."

❧ Thursday December 25

I took my small son to the zoo and when we got to the lion enclosure, the magnificent beasts were strolling up and down and looking at us looking at them.

I explained how strong and ferocious lions are and my son seemed fascinated and thoughtful.

Then he said, "Daddy, if that lion gets out of its enclosure and eats you all up, what bus will I get home?"

❧ Friday December 26

After Sunday service, an old parishioner waits to speak to the minister.

"I can tell you," she says kindly, shaking the minister's hand vigorously, "every service you give is better than the next!"

❧ Saturday December 27

My elderly mother is the most organised person when it comes to Christmas. She does everything herself.

I went with her to the Post Office to buy stamps for her Christmas cards and small parcels.

"What denomination?" asked the Post Mistress.

"Oh, my goodness," exclaimed Mother. "Well, I suppose you better give me a dozen Catholic and a dozen Presbyterian ones and a few Methodists."

⅔ Sunday December 28

I was getting my hair cut and I asked the barber when would be the best time to bring in my two-year-old son.

Without any hesitation at all, the barber answered, "When he's five."

⅔ Monday December 29

We had just moved from our rather isolated house in the country into a new block of flats in the city. Our seven-year-old son John, was very excited and woke really early. There was a safe play area with swings in the garden and I suggested he go down and play for a while. A little while later, he came back in.

"Mum – guess what," he said, "every house has its own doorbell and they all work!"

❧ Tuesday December 30

I caught my little granddaughter dipping into the sweets that came inside her bigger sister's selection box.

"You are not stealing Susie's sweeties are you?" I enquired.

"No," she replied quick as a flash, "I'm helping her share."

❧ Wednesday December 31

Famous last words: "Nice doggie!"